LIGHTING THE SHADOW

Also by Rachel Eliza Griffiths:

Mule & Pear
The Requited Distance
Miracle Arrhythmia

LIGHTING THE SHADOW

Rachel Eliza Griffiths

Four Way Books
Tribeca

Michele Antoinette (Pray) Griffiths
August 31, 1954 - July 28, 2014

Peggy S. Griffiths
April 23, 1925 - July 22, 2012

Kevin

Please direct all inquiries to:
Editorial Office
Four Way Books
POB 535, Village Station
New York, NY 10014
www.fourwaybooks.com

Library of Congress Cataloging-in-Publication Data

Griffiths, Rachel Eliza.
[Poems. Selections]
Lighting the shadow / Rachel Eliza Griffiths.
pages ; cm
ISBN 978-1-935536-57-4 (acid-free paper)
I. Title.
PS3607.R5494A6 2015
811'.6--dc23
2014030218
This book is manufactured in the United States of America and printed on
acid-free paper.

Four Way Books is a not-for-profit literary press. We are grateful for the assistance
we receive from individual donors, public arts agencies, and private foundations.

This publication is made possible with public funds from the National Endowment for the Arts

NYSCA

and from the New York State Council on the Arts, a state agency.

[clmp]

We are a proud member of the Council of Literary Magazines and Presses.
Distributed by University Press of New England

One Court Street, Lebanon, NH 03766

CONTENTS

Verses from The Dead Americans' Songbook

The Human Zoo

Notes

"We and the flowers throw shadows on the earth.
What has no shadow has no strength to live."

—Czeslaw Milosz

"When one looks from the darkness into the light, however, one sees all the
difference between here and there, this and that."

—Marilynne Robinson

"The lightning has shown me the scars of the future."

—W.S. Merwin

"But I lie down / to a different turbulence / and a plan of transformation."

—Jay Wright

The Dead Will Lead You

Across scarred meadows, red
blue, white. The star-flung sky scrapes
gold grass. Unknown milk, endless
the stone figures in the fields.
Who will embalm our bones?
Shattered inside of mythologies,
we are idols, praised by blood & sun.
You will call & listen for the children,
cradled in moonlight. Side-by-side,
their silence deranged,
deflowered by ghost primers.
Years pulse the skull,
the ashen hills, the expanse of desert
shorn with prayers. You walk alone
through mirages, museums,
eyelids, water, estuaries
where wings repeat flight
until this desire is memorized. This,
is what you must learn
by heart. The closed flesh
as commandment, a terra cotta
smear of fingerprints
praying along the blue cave.
Mercy is the pulse of lupin
in a yellow field. My mother's

eyes are forgotten vases of irises.
Lighting the shadow, a woman
crawls out beneath her own war.
Ruin, I have lived
inside your estate.
I remember the night horses
reckless with beauty
when the trembling poured
through my windows,
the animals surrounded my bed
as we floated through
the house, the world without sail,
anchor, ornament, or oar. My memory
was a painted mast, filled
with the inviolate breath
of what history can
blow apart.

| Diaphanous Corpse

"I thought the most beautiful thing in the world must be shadow, the million moving shapes and cul-de-sacs of shadow. There was shadow in bureau drawers and closets and suitcases, and shadow under houses and trees and stones, and shadow at the back of people's eyes and smiles, and shadow, miles and miles and miles of it, on the night side of the earth."

—Sylvia Plath

Woman to Lightning

after Ai

We rolled in flashes of God, fighting
pleasure as it tore
our shadows across smoke.

When we burned of life nothing was better
than our purgatory of embers.

I wanted a matchbox. A grandmother clock. I wanted the dark
house shingled in blue & bruised

wildfire. Touch me or, err.

How could I ever forget the shame on my floor,
a birthmark of you. I covered every mirror. I grieved
the squalls of our silhouettes, rising & dying. Once slave,
      I pulled my passage over the earthly gush of swells.

Revision that I was. Passing through the aviary of dead poets,
their naked bird ribs glittering with time. The universe
pressed like a coin upon their opened eyes.

Saltwater poured over joyless shoulders
as I was carried out of my life. Through blood

I sang & erased my name
until I could only name your arrows.

I've got the scars to prove it.

The nights were static & strained. I left the radio low
& returned to its amnesia each morning. America,
shining like a gun. I practiced. The barrel of my voice

aimed at thunderheads & headless saints. The volume of my life
so uneasy beneath evenings of starlight & dread.

Loneliness dragged me by my hair through back rooms
where emptied velvet chairs watched me struggle
with this blow of light.

You were happy, weren't you?

I tried to grasp the fingers slipping through
(*the smear of*)
my dreams. My footing struck clouds. I swear

I meant no harm.

But you were happy, weren't you?

Like the backhand of a palm flying
to my face.

The desire in the flying,
the wing, blurred.

Small Prayer to the God of Epiphany

You heard me ask not to be harmed.
      As if you could—
      or could
      not be harm itself—
      undressing that old speech
& so you were the waters, pulling
dead weight up. Broken words could float
      if breath was complicit.
You'd want me to unhinge, finger
by finger, the place where I held
to rock.
      Leaping from the cliff
wasn't as interesting as holding the weight of flesh
in winter air. We try to establish
      what infinity is, what eternity means—
it means there is a distinct forever
that can be calculated
never to arrive.
      I lifted my hands in the night.

The Woman and The Branch

I knew. I knew. My mother gave me
her bluebird of happiness. Carrying the glass
inside my skin to school, I was young.
Show us what you have, the world said.
I was polishing somebody's rapture.
It wasn't mine. Not my paradise
or my mother's love, but oh god
how it shone. I could never tell
which bird was singing. I went home
like a canticle to its branch. I flew
through gray leaves away from
childhood. I gave my mother answers I knew,
didn't ask whether there was another color—
was blue right after all? Was happiness
a song to be shattered?
I couldn't explain the frailty, how
the figurine had cracked
when I looked through its life.

Woman, With Her Own Crossfire

The earth within the mind
yields a paradise stoned with hills where
red-tailed gods circle
women who balance thirsting
basins of love like crowns.

Kneeling in daylight in the middle of the road,
my dress & eyes torn
back to bone, I could not leave you stranded.
I held your body against my face. My heart,
alone with the shape of your dying. The former shadow
no longer speaks & the tongue leaves
no elegy of sludge.

How to tend a corpse of love? Which wound is
the most fatal? Shame dislodging
the seahorse of a spine?

Yet I was dragging you, dead-eyed & silent,
over the stones, until I could not
distinguish whose blood left
a new road
the mimosa trees would not mourn.

In a harbor of white crosses, you were erased.
This potter's page hovers it shroud of clay
over the seal of you

my mouth
watermarked.

Let me know my scandal:

you & I,
today & the past,
time & bone,
were once simple inventions.

Let me join lightning as it welds the body
to another bridge
of infinite volume.

Let me tell you
it will be soon. The glory
of my household
filthy with stars.

My Dress Hangs There

A woman pulls night over her hips & makes the bleak seams blur the faith of her legs. If she names blood she will exist. The woman called Memory will have enough to wear in a room glazed with silk & flames. I hang my flesh on the French door as her light shakes my hunger into sequins. I'm small & scratch her heels. History stalks my body, examines my teeth, my scalp, & thighs. What can I bear for the narrative? The auction? The fondled hips of an alphabet switch partners inside a score I won't follow. My dance card filled before my birth. Will I scale my story? In the middle of a city I am between years of ruin. My eyes walk the street below while my shadow dangles between the Hotel of Impossible and the Hotel of Mocking Words. There is my tongue near the curb where a woman's shadow is feeding a songbird. There are the curling night scrolls of my hair. The feathers I once wore at my ears pause midair as if listening. A tomcat swaggers past a storefront holding a piece of my cheek in its mouth. It's early & the workmen whistle, coaxing sunlight from their pitches of tar. The men look up at the world & hold the sky by its own throat. They beg the dawn to leap over night's skull. *Dream me a woman,* they say to Memory. Above, the other woman who is History never kneels in the sightless canals of pleasure. She will never eat bribes or pay twice for her mistakes or affairs. The hearts she buries are anonymous & she gathers them against their will. This woman can have any life she wants. Any defeat. *Do you want my life*, I say. My voice is a gold streetlamp corroded by ghost moths. The victory is always the same. Across the room I watch the moonlight flicker in her unlit breasts. *Beg me to take your life away. Beg for me like a man*, she says. The height of desire as it falls to day.

(Mexico City, 2010)

Disarming of Shadow, Arming of Light

I wish I were like Johnny Cash
& thought my heart was mine.

I've worn a black suit
my entire life. It suits the war
my eyes ignite.

My sins sit on my lap,
bald, blind, desperate
for the mercy of lost roads,
glottal white lines.

Only smoke will take me
far to nowhere—

a woman living
between
her own burning road

& a charmed God—

the unmarked sky
where a plague of blackbirds

fell across my back
like an unlit cross.

The Reckoning of Relics

This is the gristle of imagery. The need to see what is past.
Not history, not the Before or Long Ago, but the saint's finger,
the sarcophagus of imagery, the immortal phrases of
headstones. Somewhere after death, a detail remains.
Sits in the mind, brightly impenetrable as a mineral:
lapis lazuli or diamond. It was June in Austerlitz
& I was circling the stalls of my life,
flinging kerosene over what I'd done wrong.
The stars slid over hummingbirds in the evening.
Deer neared me, then turned away
in the meadow's lumina. Beneath apple trees
I sat & rubbed my hands across the bark
of my own skin & the red compass within my ribcage.
One afternoon Peter walked me through Millay's house,
asked me to imagine the house, the woman's work, the masks.
I was staying in the barn, invisible from her windows,
taking a month to heal the broken flames
of my phoenix, the better woman prepared for flight.
I walked for hours, miles, became a vapor,
returned from ash, wrote to Tracy, climbed trees,
met black snakes & barred owls, breathed
like a firefly. Alone, a frame of light
in a museum, without a painting inside,
without a self-portrait.
In the morning high grass floated

beneath dew & I listened to
my new flesh: the truer poem.
The listening saved me.
Even when my ears bled & my heart leaked.
I stood at the window in my head
& looked out at the loping black bear,
the pinions of black crows, the thickets
of youth flattening beneath my whispers.
Upstairs Peter held his palm out to me,
the hush & eternity of a dead woman's curls,
faded with threads of red.

(Steepletop, 2012)

Elegy

"Cut my shadow from me.
Free me from the torment
of seeing myself without fruit."
Federico Garcia Lorca

The night has let go of me & touches the barren grave
where my shovel works. The poems are stony beds, inscribed
imperfectly. They are also loaves & lovers. Dear *enfants,*
the cradle starves & I wander
across the god-flecked bridge between night valleys.
The meadows in the old country are sawdust.
The moon douses my hair & peels my breasts. The sun
forgets me, leaves no gold treasure
on my hips. Memory is a burnt child
I carry on my back. All of the hours refuse to stay longer
when the last glass of Bordeaux
runs out of the house, clutching its belt.
My secrets have chapped lips. Once I gave them honey,
blood, & language. I never inquired of their subtle pain.
Why should I want their torment? Why do I believe in fools?
Now I see gardens wherever roots were pulled up.
A smile of quiet wheat thrives in the ash of mud. A seed
shaped like youth blown backwards. I close the gate
& switch on every light
my flesh has needed. Even the tongue

in my mouth, diluted
by farewell, shines with the love
of letting go.

Fragments of Poems Returned by Sender

You were waving when I looked back.
When I scraped winter from my flesh
& mimicked the silence of geese,
bruised arrows skimming grief.

Somewhere I moved beneath trees.
I'd love to name their limbs for you
but can't you see past all that? Anatomy
says we're all the same.
Symmetry, flawed by soul, errata,
elegy & so forth.

I was crawling across lawns,
feral & flattened
into lies & scored lines,
dive bars & overtures.
In the dark I swung my legs
across the wooden prows
of men & women lost at sea,

the misery
of a jukebox, paid & repetitive.
Appreciated for nostalgia

alone. Closer now is the absence
of snow. Because it is summer
& the heat unfastens like a black dress
around my legs. My dark cries
claw the dance floor.

Give me a call,
let me know how you're doing,
I write to my friends
from the hospital
in a common gown of birds.

Somewhere resembles you
but it is not a location. There is no point
where the map picks up
the sum of oceans. The grid's ablutions
raised over blue madness,

the symmetry of absence
in a mirror with no one
looking.

Native Fire

A woman burns in the socket of midnight. She opens the door of a house she once abandoned. Where the men had taken her, walking her into the kitchen while they made her light their torches. A woman in her own passage, she looks up at the sky from her own belly where she turns & melts like evening. *The dark is warm*, she tells the ash that falls from the sky all year round. Next to her body the pulse of a secondhand memory fades until the red turns brown. She taps the window of the earth's dreams. She makes a door with her breath and falls through a blue field of ocean. Sister of Icarus, step-daughter of Oshun. The ghost ships in the river do not speak as she beats her wing, her belly of ashes heavy as clouds. *Life is taking something away*, she thinks, holding Leda in her arms as the swan's shadow leaves them alone again. The distant music of her house crackles. But this is right, this homelessness she has made with paint, flight, & bitter honey. Her body floats in its oil of silence. *Life gives us everything so that there is really no choice.* Slowly, over her shoulders, dawn is the anonymous mouth that rips her spine apart.

July 13, 1954

"I live on air, accepting things as they come."
Frida Kahlo

Because you sat upright, not yet
ash. Already myth, yes,
already. Spine broken into bone silence.
You sat upright near fire,
preparing as the phoenix must
gather her fires to die. Lady Lazarus
whispering inside your silence.
Fitting the body into lightning,
the faces, painted & photographed,
a furnace of dreams wait in paradise.
Because we gathered around your ribs,
your hundreds of convex embraces
& dignities. Near the immortal needle
of desire you'll twist perpetually,
out of reach in paint, pleasure.
Blazing, your night hair & soft
bones descend through the canopy
to kiss your coverlet of skin.
I never write an elegy for you, Frida.
But once in late spring I lingered
in a sky of laments
at the top of the stairs in your house.

The last room. On the last day
a young man with eyes like burning
told me *She is still here*, he said,
pointing out the urn, shaped & brown
like a humble creature of the earth,
glazed by the hands of a tarnish
that glazes anything worthwhile. Animal, which?
Pre-Columbian, two clay arms extended
to hold your fatted death & afterlife life.
*I don't always tell where
she is*, he said in Spanish, his voice
splitting like a fruit. Frida,
there is a death mask of your face
on the canopied bed. Above, God
waits like a mirror. In the corner
the painted leg in its red boot
waiting to dance.
I am talking to you,
naming comets
& my deaths in your name.

Home, A Photograph

I can light a match in the window
where a woman stands
within a cadaver of silence.
The wind of nothing
pushes through bone
frames & flypaper studded
with dying. The stillborn brick.
Childhood is a torn animal
left out of doors. Buried
beneath the porch
with treasures & baby teeth.
The tomatoes that never grew.
My face hides in the mud
cellar near broken lights.
The skin of walls, widowed.
Where canopies folded
into fists & prayers.
Inside the eaves
of the body, a bird
slams its song
against flight.
Where the laughter
spilled & burnt like sugar

in a hearth
of visions no one
could set free.

Another Woman's Coat

for J.H.

Alone with snowfall & pockets
of silence beneath shining streetlamps,
I pull her coat closer, finding spaces
in its arms. These seams do not belong
to me. And I won't know this yet—
slipping along snowy Remsen. I stop
on the Brooklyn Promenade. I'm solitary
again & stare at the city lining the river.
Against air, I pull the hood down,
burrow inside her wordless
flesh. Alive from dancing
with friends & the music
of that pulled over me
like an eyelid of glitter.
Can Manhattan's insect
windows make me out
on the other side of its veins?
Gatsby's green heart
of a wish. Or whatever
was above me
that looked at my mouth
in the dark & said
Yes, that's enough, isn't it?
Blinking, immeasurable
in snow that needles
like fire, I'll walk,

a Siamese with ten shadows,
amongst dense brownstones.
Heart, what joy inscribes your telescope?
Snow light growing the shadows
of sycamores & fire hydrants
into giants. The bare pine seller
stands. The streetlights change
for nothing. When I get to my door
I'll reach for a key
that opens & returns me
to myself like a rune. Then I see
I'm wearing a coat
that isn't mine. Her syllables
& smiles & the wit of another
woman's neck lingering
in the lining. Sweet-strange
& irony & how you couldn't
tell in the dark, you could wear
something so intimate
& otherwise? Hearing her
hands & breasts & ribs
murmur inside of the down.
The feathers you now
warm with your own
body. Inseparable

as the music we shared
as we danced,
the holiday like flecks
of tinsel caught under
the god's tongue. Julie,
I hope you'll forgive
me for wanting to
verse your instrument,
& how, when Brooklyn
wasn't looking, I made
angels against the air,
our skin, like words slipped back
before midnight & knowing
I have no other way
to bear my life, you
laugh at the café
where we meet
& tell me
when we give
our coats back
with wonder
for ourselves
that the dance
was so lovely
your legs hurt
in the morning.

July 22, 2012

On the ferry to Governor's Island I don't recognize New York.
Great & blinding, the buildings are close enough
for the boat to scrape their glitter. A small feeling
vibrates behind my eyes. Beneath the day's tripwire, a circuit
of grief quivers, unseen, too small to be a speck. I hear it
as I'm blinking against another summer. I'm thirty-three.

I'm twenty-eight. I'm sixteen, seventy-one. Nine, two,
          a kingdom of caves where hags & diamonds wait to wake,
to be found. Find me. The light around me leaps & goes
wherever the gulls flash above the waves. There is the Queen Anne's
lace of a child's laugh, the froth of the ferry's wake, the man
patting his bicycle like a pet. Our shadows racing
          the surface of old water.

A little finch of infinity makes its way through the blue interior.
New York floats like a promise on its back. It's going to go
fast: immortality. It will be difficult to make out
above the electric melt of dreams.

     Read a poem about Brooklyn's bliss, about this blessing, our *blessure*,
          then turn your sail of oblivion
                    toward the surprises life endures.

Breathe & sing or don't. You'll stop anyway. Tumbling
from your perch on earth. You'll stop singing blood
        & papering your cages. You'll stay put like a night dream.

At the festival of poets there's a machine in the center
of the great lawn where poets can ride a toy carousel. Beyond the ghost
barracks & the house where half the roof of solitude
      is burned
& cracked from someone's indiscretion.

                There is the spoil of beauty & that way
auroras beneath the life brood
above us. In the circle of the stalls, misshapen
& shining, the irony

    the blackbird studies inside stanzas
eludes its own songs.

           I wear a white dress & my throat is clean
with what the sun has been saying since summer began:

                      there is no place
that does not see you.

And what I do not know
is that mockingbird offering its intractable arias to me

                              & none will hear its affectations

but those who have received
its dolorous shriek of farewell.

I'll have lost the sensation of what any useful word can give
the body. I'll have lost that when I hear
the funeral of my father's voice
announcing what that bird of paradise
had been trying to make me see.

The stars do not want your sharp indecision or agony.
            You get in the car with your sister, your brother, the man
                  who will bury you with love. The husband who will lie
                        in stone by your side, your dusts merging
                                          like glitter.

The whole way he touches your hand in the dark.

Grandmother, it is old & long & cold with its one-sided window. That's death.
Do you sense my fingertips there on your shoulder where it is still a little warm?
The herd bumps invisibly. Dogs, jackals, lambs. The temples where I kneel
in smoke. Dogs, jackals, lambs. Eating my grief, the meat of it new
while animals push me back in the air with their shoulders. Our nostrils flare
with the scent of what was living & what is left.

Inside this weakness I am spit. Refuse to feed at the throat of elegy.
I'm too obedient. *Let her go,* my mother says at the foot of the body.
        I can't, I can't, I can't. I'm so angry at the golems of death
I'll wait my turn & woo my Furies. I'll hunt, my howls magnificently robed
        in vowels & photographs. Won't skip the line, the mindful
break down, starve
the snow.

O fool of a woman, of a poet, & granddaughter
I must be & now not be. Fool.

Look at the face where I was
contained & my father & the seasons the temples
cannot feel because they are spared & sacred.

We are left the words of things
like a family of wolves folding their lips to scream
in a pasture of weak flowers &

        I still had Love to say, things
of no importance to mutter.

                        Desire turns its open face to me.
                        Its eyes are scarlet pools. The mouth
                        is a flower that will kill me
                        unless I ravage,
                        etch a poultice of syllables.

I kiss & kiss & kiss & kiss
the supremacy of this thought:

                        a second blooming that will bear
                        my grandmother's life back to me,
                        make me unborn, & my father
                        just a breeze
                        inside of a young woman's hand.

36

Vergüenza

Woman, I wish I didn't know your name.
What could you be? Silence in my house
& the front yard where the dogwood
wouldn't make up its mind about flowers.
A world cringes, half-fallen, half-
shadowed beneath a torque of rain.
I too am leaving. I too am half-spun.
The other day near the river
I bent down & Narcissus
turned his immaculate mouth
from mine, refusing to caress
my howls. Silence in the trees
all around the shotgun house & that scent
of cedar whenever I dream.
I turn the light around on the ground,
sweeping the red mud, holding
the lightning like a rattler. Like a hood of
poison, fitted over my face. Cobra
woman, slicked with copperheads.
I too am misunderstood. My face born
in a caul of music. Bravado.
The men come into the yard
& pull all my clothes off,
walk me into the house,
into my own kitchen.

Tell me not to say
say I'm wrong.

Self, Traction

"The lightning has shown me the scars of the future."
W.S. Merwin

They pull the woman up in her bed. New bandages clasp her face in white. They pull her legs down because she is trying to fly. Beneath wounds you will find water. Skin, lust, longing are strokes of faith. They pull the woman up in her bed. Moonlight seduces the death flaring in her eyes. They pull her legs down then pull her dress away to shame her thorns. Pull God out of the folds of her skin. They do not let her thoughts peal her head. Her tears sculpt a world. They pull the woman up in their bed. She has been moved to her grave to make them feel more comfortable. Beneath the gauze her breasts flutter, stuffed with starlings & the ecstasy of cobalt pigment. She is a cardinal lost in the hive of language. Her song has no pain but offers mercy anyway. They place a stone beneath her teeth. Dare her to bear down on black roots & shatter. In agony & goldleaf, she laughs. They push the body to the edge of the bed to study their incisions. It is a wick, the body they want to drag through fire. Effigy. They pull the woman up in her bed, not liking her sounds because she is free. *A mind is a socket in lightning when it flies*, I said. They pull the light out of her skin, pull the lilac out of her skull, pull the poems, wet & writhing, out of her, wringing the body in opposite directions until the line is perfectly straight.

(Coyoacán, Mexico, 2010)

| A Dark Race for Enlightenment

"And I listen for everything because I know it won't always be so.
I listen too closely and sometimes the listening gets too loud."

—Edwidge Danticat

Recurrence

Next to the throne where we are waiting
for your judgment I stand behind your hardback chair.
I don't tie you to its broken arms. Your arms, already wooden.
I don't offer you the torture of patience. I don't offer you
confession. Freedom. You could only give me
what you gave the scholars. A chamber of vapors
you named History.
I give you water. You do not see my blood in it.
We have not tasted pleasure for centuries.
I swivel a tambourine like a word through air
when you insist that I am useless. The music of bells
salvages the wreck of your splendor.
We nod in time to airless trumpets. I watch the scales
of love tilt. I touch your hip & you like that.
You like my bones to want you.
In a solo you know the harmonies that make me
shiver. My lips cold with song & blood.
Are those your lips? Are you smiling?
God & Justice sit at a near table, peel
oranges. Eat chicken & drink wine. Play
tonk & bullshit. War. Their burning scales
& blindfolds pushed back. A bucket
of ears sits atop the Bible. A capuchin
studies the players' hands & takes coins beneath
the table as they move toward each other

like amiable battleships. A radio screeches.
Below us cities unfurl their white flags
& the earth heaves with melting.
I have polished you with my hair. I shine you
with my leather rag of syllables. It's all I am.
I give you fruit after tasting each seed
for knowledge. "Here is a book about war," I say
& you smile, taking it from my bloody hands.
In the government of dreams you are behind
on your paperwork. So you are like democracy.
You offer me your seat. I have been standing
here for over two hundred years. By your side,
against you. Even when you left me
for another woman. The smell of me
singed the sky & the harvest ate
my ashes. I wait for your orders.
I'm starving. Mushroom, nimbus,
tornado, tsunami. Fire. Fire. Fire.
I hold a sterling tray of faces
waiting for you
to make up your mind.

26

Your names toll in my dreams.
I pick up tinsel in the street. A nameless god
streaks my hand with blood. I look at the lighted trees
in windows & the spindles of pine tremble
in warm rooms. The flesh of home, silent.
How quiet the bells of heaven must be, cold
with stars who cannot rhyme their brilliance
to our weapons. What rouses our lives each moment?
Nothing but life dares dying. My memory, another obituary.
My memory is a cross. Face down. A whistle in high grass.
A shadow pouring over the sill of calamity.
Your names wake me in the nearly dark hour.
The candles in our windows flicker
where your faces peer in, ask us
questions light cannot answer.

(December 2012)

Woman, New Delhi

When the wheel turns
from the paved country, the angels
strain like mosquitos on the windshield.
The men force the woman's friend
to watch as they pull off
the wings of her skin.
When only God may look
at the blur within &
know there is nothing
greater to forgive.

(December 2012)

I Select My Jury Before Justice Appears

You made things up. How you felt. Who you were.
Beyond the cities & the caves, you sent me to look
for your body. You hid yourself, disguised your taste,
your voice. In our mouths you planted longing & hunger.
We walk around repeating your hands.
We can say who is wrong & who is nothing.
We polish the sidewalks with our forgetting,
play the lotto, bum noise from the dead, turn
our mothers & fathers into obelisks.
We won't abandon the orphans of history,
or the worship of their shivering.
Lift our workhorses & smear our senses
with dogma. You made things up.
How we felt.
And now emptiness is the feeling we trust best.
We walk around mourning our germs.
You unmade the houses
we tended, the unfinished children, the lonely flat tv.
There was a chance to shatter. The detour
of loving then dying
too devastating to follow.
The gavel, the injury of a cross.
And we look up to what?
The alchemy of perpetual discontent.
To ask for what?

Occupy Flower

"One more word like this, and the hammers
will swing over open ground."
                    Paul Celan

I tore a blooming through the streets.
Light attached to the seismic lid of tides. I tore & tore.
Here is a sentence wrapped in stinging.
The jaundiced ash of the dead riding
their own courage. Mutiny murmurs the pistil
& the stem. My tongue is your treaty.
Whatever did you want from us but rain?
I tore over the earth, racing
like a star. I remember how it once was
when the world waited. On either seam
of seeing I am folded into a vision
I cannot dream.
My longing is deferred, as a loan
or lover. Give way to the evidence,
rising over the great house
behind the trees. The hunter's bow
is distant. It is breaking the sower's
body. Give way to the root
stalking our lives. Here is the America—
they asked us to exist in gold,
the currency of a terrible trust.

Elegy

I remember the boys & their open hands. High fives
      of farewell. I remember that the birches waved too,
            the white jagged limbs turning away from incessant wildfires.

The future wavered, unlike a question, unlike
      a hand or headstone. The future moved & the fields already knew it.

I remember the war of the alphabet, its ears sliced from its face. I
      know that language asks for blood.

The children of kudzu, lilac, the spit of unknown rivers. I remember the jury
      & the judge of the people. The buckshot that blew
            the morning's torso into smoke.

That last morning I begged the grandmothers to leave their rage next to red candles
      & worn photographs of their children & their blue-eyed grandson
           with his bleeding heart. The savior bled flowers.

I scattered the stones the trees bore. Gray vultures came for my children.
      They knew the old country better than me. They broke through
           skyscrapers & devoured both villain & hero.

& boys were pouring, wanted & unwanted & missing yet from the long mouth
      where their voices were forced to say they were nothing. But they were men,
                           invisible

& native & guilty beyond their glottal doubt.

I remember calling out to the savage field where more boys knelt & swung
through the air. I remember how their eyes rolled back
in blood, milk, & gasoline. Their white teeth
chewing cotton into shrouds, scars, & sheets.

They gave me their last words. They gave me smiles for their fathers.
They slept in my arms, dead & bruised. Long as brambles.

The bullets in their heads & groins
quieting like a day. The meat of nothing.

I held their million heads in my lap when the bodies were taken away.
I don't know if what's left will dance or burn.
I wash their eyelids with mint.

But let God beg pardon to them & their mothers

& I don't know if the body is a pendulum of where love cannot go
when the tongue is swollen with the milk of black boys.
I pulled their lives from the trees & lawns & schools.
The unlit houses & the river. Their forewings wet
with clouds

& screaming. I won't leave them,

        huddled like bulls inside the stall of a word. I am the shriek,

              the suture, the petal

                    shook loose from their silence.

Anti Elegy

The faces of our death are unresolved. The body, identified, is
        confirmed by music. Rag time. Big band blood. We all look alike.
              We're prayers. The coroner's baby grand piano
                 in a cold drawing room.

We were not identified by our teeth [broken] or by our country [broken].
        These are the words we will not be.
              Will you finish this poem or give the back of its mouth
                    to the gun?

The hearts, terra cotta blue, were buried beneath birch.
        Drop bread from the hands that push sentences into our cages.
           Murder the grooms & Apollos. Drag your chariots
              over the head of Orpheus
                 where a headless agony rolls
                    like a kickball in a Jasper road.

The business of caretakers? Bet on that
        staying platinum. The more black you buy & bury
           the harder heaven shines its pennies.

Bless this nation of uncertain chambers. Bludgeon the orchestra with blues.
Plastic bags of glory going for a name on any corner

where a pick-up game distracts the night from the black
bruise swinging in the jaundice of a streetlight.

The metaphors grieve their own offspring. The riddles are tired of numbers
& bony ghettos. The scandal of marrow
as it witnesses our gaze. The crap game

of bones in repose.

Before Blood After Honey

for Mahmoud Darwish

Give me a tongue that cannot translate memory into air. Narrative is no enemy of bone. This is the story mud has learned. The eye laves red. And the ear totters like a crow in its hearing, an abyss of black opening sound into air. I am giving you the image of our insides splayed like wings in daylight. I am giving you the opposite of the negative, which is fire. The shrapnel of our teeth devours what we taste but cannot imagine. What we must wound first (the skin) to feed what is beyond.

For a moment our story is anonymous as a child's head rolling like an olive in the vineyard. Who made these gorgeous vines & the beauty that is nearly malevolent? For the length of the sky a city eats every citizen. In the next instant we brace only for the shatter of the bowl of wine or tears, the ferment of pressure.

I am behind the rows of women who will be opened & burned like letters. And so the flesh rolls against splendid sweetness. A stain of honor left to dry on the stones. The exile of love wanders the passage of my eyes. In the body we have known a sunken garden of miracles. The amber smoke from centuries lingers in the honeycomb.

Our scale is set & armed for oblivion.

I wait for you. Light happens finally beneath the skin. I kick my head through the trees & chase the air that is left. I wait & then sail forward on the froth of twilight. I wait & you remember I am the marrow.

Elegy, Interior Figures

*"Go, go, go said the bird: human kind
Cannot bear very much reality."*
                                    T.S. Eliot

You did not matter
in the gospel of salted eyes.
You rose & fell in the birth
light of farewell. In that fire
I flung your burnt head
into air. *Breathe*, I said
without dissatisfaction.
Against briars I rubbed
your lips & pride.
Do not speak again
of the intentions
great poets wear
attached to the unseen
brims of their helmets,
their rose-rot skulls.
Across fields of shadows
I carried you as I galloped.
Dragging my mind
like a hoof in blue clay.
Crows watched. The blackbird
God. You left a trail of dying
like a soldier or poet. We ordered

our dreams to be ready
at dawn. We retreated to stonewalls
where you would be
exposed. Where men's hands itched
to draw our blood from rock.
Against element, syllable, home.
Where you would know
thirst & sunlight always.
Where time & bone would collapse
anything that made us brave.
I could not welcome you after death.
Spinning under the fist
& fire of love, the music
I could not sing
when you gave up.

Human Ceremony with Watermelon Sugar

after Richard Brautigan

I meet a figure on the shore. Lily,
sulfur, & fire. The settlements on the ridge—
who lived there? Flame, ballast,
& grains. Flower & cinder whorl
in the froth. Sometimes, irony,
not quite idiot. Who were they?
Unwise sapiens, swaying
in the smudge of light?
Also, it was about faith & iDeath
& how the burning polished the soul.
Yes, soul. It was beneath that,
wasn't it? What fire did they wear
when they promised one another
some relic of eternity? The Forgotten Works?
The ledge of death between those dunes
where tigers play guitars & sing.
Paper blowing. Star, spit, sugar. The contrition
of ethers. Finally, I will meet you
at the trout's lip, my tongue,
mollusk & petal, my shellacked words,
all blown back
like the dead thrown
from our overturned boat.

The Year in Pictures

1.

I wash Bob Kaufman's face
with my hair. I press my fingers into the crosses
made of Band-Aid tape he has arranged
in verse on his face, a cartography
of manifests. I carry his *Ancient Rain*
with me as I descend
into a photograph of a factory
in Bangladesh.

2.

In the dark a thick-eyed whip
of a man
attempts to shoot an apple
from the light of my head. Bob says,
"Baby, you're dreaming of Burroughs, that's all he does—
shoot up, so don't worry. My face is cleaner
than Jesus. Paradise's unmarked here.
Loneliness gains you discovery.
Leave apples & sadness & freedom
alone. That's all junk. Shooting up
your head in the mirror." He's a euphonic
horn, all Bird & beatnik voodoo. Bebop.
But this year in pictures is ruin, Bob,

& the ancient rain & crowded solitude.
Dare the universe when it's all
finished like a Basquiat. *Nothing
to be gained here.*

3.
In Taslima's picture I can't shake
the explosion from my eyes.
To see a man
clutching a woman, a single cry
of blood squeezed from his closed clay
eyes. The pale flower on her pink sari
glows like a bloom in a dying
lapel. The workers sewed & plucked
thread. The wrecked labor
crushed bones to gunpowder.
Across the world I tear my eyes
like gauze. I wear the machines.

The dead man listened for her
heart beneath the heap. How long
could he hear her love? The silent
tremor of her golden bangle
bracelet in the dark

while she prayed in dust. I'm howling,
but Ginsberg's gone
away. The workers' lives rolled
like Lazarus beneath cheap stones.
The lovers must have shared meals
under a buzzing bulb. Peeling fruit
& hope, they clung to their wheels
& steaming windows. They had to
eat.

4.
I hold a photograph
of a building over my face.
Is it a museum already, is it
Congress, a riddled schoolhouse,
is it a synagogue, a Sikh temple,
is it a brownstone, or a basement
where three women cared for a baby
while they were raped, kept as hostages,
is it the world bank or shopping mall in Africa, is it
276 flowers pleading for their parents,
is it a movie cinema, is it
your own head blown to oil,
is it always to be terror? Was it full

of rooms you helped somehow
to destroy because you did not
know? A boy whose hair resembled fire
walked into a theater in Aurora & fired?
Is it the one who shot his mother
four times in the head & went out
the front door to school
where little children listened
in sunlight for the bell?

5.
The clock never settles its hands
in the image. The hands never raise an alarm
for the workers. All of us
strain to get the life
finished, revised, the flesh
in proper fit to soul. Never
enough silk or needle.

6.
Forgotten, as if you never were
a person, or a text…forgotten

In a photograph I see myself, a soldier
adorned in love & honor, standing beside
my shell-smooth wife. The roses
she holds in torment, the shock
of her veil. I have my face,
hands, fingers, & part of
my skull. Yesterday melts
over our nuptials. Her absence
formal & stiff
as a uniform.

I see myself in war photographs
from World War II. My shoe
alone in the background
folded like an ear. Trapped
in the leathery smoke of bodies
weeping as they cool.

7.
Can I hold them tightly
on my page, wrap their ribs
with bowels of paper? Syllables
in a mass morgue, unidentified
& amputated. Consumed by garments

& hours of impossible conditions,
I see their lives as clearly as a sleeve.

Schoolchildren slicing apples
with glittering eyes.
A pink dress & blue shirt singing
on the line, clean & alive
as daylight.

"a word of rescue from the great eyes"

where violence interrupts the assault
of language & ligaments, where they connect as a third rail
       of sparks, blue & wide like welts of stars

the transfusion of imagery & vernacular
& the deep slurs of silence
following the echo

    of any final word,

        the scraped bowl

    ~

            : muriel :

a man knocked me to the floor
of Grand Central Station, no reason
visible but the blue-gold fortune above,
the constellations backwards, the dead
inventor insisting on "divine perspective,"

& so the stars too were frozen
in the high green dome
of trains & schedules,

lost loves, heaps
of shelled oysters, the great clock—

I remember how the book of Jarrell flew
            through the scissoring legs of women
wearing heels & thin regrets
their bitter smell of ache & coffee

the fall drew my blood out of me, out of the book,
& my lip burst though I said nothing

when my knees scraped the rail-hard ground, &
my head cracked
against the newsprint bin & sludge

& the man saying
nothing his open hand
could say better

come & touch me, I said. come & try
to get inside of here. the mythology turned
away, cat-eyed, the spotted trees
prostrate in the storm. even the animals have left
here. the silence roams & the news
rustles the genesis of history's black hole.

        ~

> *"The lamp of the body is the eye.*
> *It follows that if your eye is clear,*
> *your whole body will be filled with light."*

        ~

"Lucille McKay, I will see you again—"

I name you here, my great-grandmother

& think of you more tonight than the others who are dead & visit me.
Their mouths orphaned, lonely as blossoms. Your pearl hair stained your
spine, pulling our story into its shadow of continents. You were buried in a
sky blue dress. Clip-on pearls riveted to consonants. Too much rouge, the
silenced blush, is what they do to women who are freed inside their own
faces. The undertaker tried his best with your peace. *Did you ever have*

that? My great-grandmother's name means light, means bloodlines eroded along Virginia rocks & Tennessee country. Her sisters passed. She was the last one. I once tangled a hard comb in her white hair.

> In the dream, my great grandmother said yes,
> > there will be another

> Lucille, in a field of white snow
> > blushing with the flash of red foxes,
> the blessing of the boats.

Muriel,

I discovered where they hid—
> the gods on the north side of the mountain
> & demanded the return of my sins to myself—

I'll carry all this & something better one day, I said
> & watched a beating of monarchs

> the orange & black blurs forced

> into my own burning

Miss Lucille said, "you can be a seeing woman

      if you want," she said, "see," & opened her palm
along my own fingers. The opaque sight
arrived & she sang Billie Holiday to her husband
the whole time
while I made an image of her joy

      & then the oldest grace came to surface, & the hand waved
through my dreams after she left, coming back
                  sometimes to laugh & pray my eyes
open when I refused to release my leash of fear

"somebody in here is so sad," she once said.
"who is that," she said above the crowns of dogs in the great forest.
"somebody in here is so blue I can hear it."

Later, she planted her palm against mine
& smiled her Lucille-smile, "you must remember—"

      & she said, "tell me what You you saw Before"

"she could see the peril of an

unexamined life.
she closed her eyes, afraid to look for her
authenticity
but the light insists on itself in the world;"

when the mountain inverted its immeasurable depth & the gods
      could not exhume the music they buried inside of my elegies
the woman I'd become & buried, the woman I'd dragged
through the long river & the streets, trying to love her
      (while her head rolled)
through pyramids, asylums, & pig alleys, hunted like a chrysanthemum

when I tried to give my life away
the women came to me
& pinned me against the snow until I was blank

when I dreamed of crawling, returning
to my mother & my father, all

      of the shredded flecks of me

     we never suspected as we passed through our birthright
of hours & days, their own childhoods spread out

next to mine into pieces

of a carnal jigsaw

I lifted my own hands I lifted my own hands I lifted
my own hands how
in the god
how like & of god
& likeness of the
& what god &

in the film about the earth colliding with a blue sphere called Melancholia
        one woman shivered & wept while the other blinked inside
                her own lucid house, her inevitable eyelids & hands thin
                    as the astonishing promise of oblivion

have you seen the unnamed hands piling upon autumn
or the waves of silverfish, the white squares of prayer
blowing along stained strings in a ghost town

we all remember departing

& being lost & trying
to return & say it was west of paradise, no
no, the other way actually . . .

> . . . to kneel
> at the center
> of the universe's plexus,
> divinity in the gut
> of our mornings

Exiled from my own women
    by the mask my mother gave me
    by the words my flesh took for silk
    by the dance of the god's unfulfilled hungers

Exiled from the loves I ruined,
    an atheist, a transvestite of syntax, an ambassador
        suffused in lost & broken splendor
Exiled from the narrative,
        my head frozen with sorrow,
    I am not Salome's utterance,

71

the gold platter tarnished with whatever
            her suitors devoured—the ice of the myth

torn back like a girl's staring mouth, torn open
        by the life desire fails

to navigate. The red & yellow water at sunset.

                        The leaving of all that.

The kings crawl in the fields, their heads hidden in the sight of gold.
Gold crown against scythe, Jean-Michel. Who but the Lord
        & the starving angels
            look at the little lambs with kindness?

In any language to speak
        is to behead the urchin-black spines of our dreams
            rolling beneath the water, enveloped
                in the narrow broth of light

                        (the marrow of leaving your head behind)

: Lucille, how wild :

the sorrow a swarm of hours
the joy as the hive
the men & the women who led the water back to me & remembered
the words & the pictures opening & shutting me inside their freedom
the inventions & the mothers & the grandmothers
the songs that live beneath the crab-rattles of battlefields
the body who looks up from road & bullet
the frog who eats the swallows
the swan falling dead across a boy's poem
the shoes piled in a vigil of suffering
the loon's cry skidding across a hidden lake
the lovers were right & wrong enough in symmetry

: how guilty, Muriel :

the phonemes feel, floating in the ether
of imagined ablution

in the film about gravity a woman spun within a smaller universe
enveloped in stars, trapped in her flesh—
she worried she was drifting

after the men left her, the woman wakened
         on the shoulder of a road outside of London
after the bite marks on her wrists vanished
after the visit to Bath & the regal crescent that opened to stars & stones
after the pills slipped into her drink by the kind doctors
after the other women told her to lie, to forget, to eat, to harbor gratitude
         instead of shame & hatred for killers & thieves
after she stood up, her flesh ripped to the bone like a solstice in winter

                 there was a field of yellow flowers waiting
                 no rain for hours
                 there was nothing she had not known before
                 no name for those flowers, the cadmium yellow angels
                         bending namelessly toward the dense earth

                         or what she could tell the authorities

about the long clouds ribboning

the rapeseed field or the woman
         burning inside of a jasmine-white fear

                                        for having survived

                              ~

after writing nothing sharing none of it
            with her own mind
she saw it in her palms, clear as rivers
                  when she touched the lips & words of other women
      who were free

& now you must believe me
            because I am telling you first,
                        because I am floating this giddy anti-iambic line
            out to you, to the deep

                        & the marrow

                        of my unquiet water where I dive
                              with my dark joy,

I tell you *it will all be enough,*
as I am enough

| Verses from the Dead Americans Songbook

"Sometimes what I feel has a difficult name.
Sometimes it is like the world before America…"

—Terrance Hayes

| new world

They are all walking in a line
back to old times. On their backs
they carry children & computers. On their heads
they balance old & new & never before.
Darling, it's a hard drive. You can touch it.
The indignity is in our heroes' shoes. Look at that one's
black-green toe sticking out of these questions.
Questions that run ahead like bald dogs.
Security is a bankrupt woman. Her misery smashed
into a suitcase fused to the bones in our hands.
The great trains arrive, late & cheap & breathless.
The fillings in their teeth are made of steam.
A ghost mare waits in a field of ghost clover.

The men took off their belts.
The women took off their eyes.
The daughters asked for confession.
There was no honor to destroy.
Children drank their futures.
The women placed their veils inside.
Inside the banks, no brilliance hid.

There were dream paintings from four centuries.
The horses grazed on spears
of carrots. The crude peace, everlasting
for study, for wonder.

Where are the men who chiseled rock
with their terror? Where did the stones break
the body? Rockefeller? Where is John Henry
buried, his bones as blue as the penitentiary
of lost ballads behind bars? Go down, man.
Henry Ford & dear Detroit. The bankrupt
Madoff gears, the rusted shank of scams.
Where is New Orleans & her tambourine
of souls? The ghost music of the big
band stick carried softly by the old presidents
& the hate-struck bullet plucked
from Malala's spirit?

Walking around in my head, I'm being
watched by my own watchdogs.
How many seasons
do you intend on adding to this
rag-to-wishes list
of things-to-forget?
Get into this rhythm, time
of heretic, truth of
lunatics. I've got a coil of
lightning & the sky is hungry
for your marquee of marrow.
Time collapses like two bodies
after a duel of love.

Didn't the tabloids show us
life on another planet
where we could look
over at the earth,
smothered in its atmosphere
of kitsch?

Didn't you wince when you became an alien?

Outside & borderless, illegal
rain shoving our complicity
to its knees. Debris sways
like a narrative from bougainvillea
in bloom. History in blossom?
Turn around this same-sex
lyric of torn silk & cover
the fuchsia hoods singing
with something thicker
than absence.

An entire expanse filled with fossils
from the caravan. Who were they?
Those Americans in bonnets
& unmade faces? High-browed,
black, blackened, smudged

by the plains & gallows
of hope & its bloody spray. Lost,
lost in wide yellow drifts. They poured,
like words from a casket, the mouth
of the indentured dead.

What light ravaged their minds?
Biting & sucking, suckling such fulfilling
articulations. And, again—

how useful they seemed.

To themselves? Thunder
& shuffle. The sale of the plea
bargain they made. Broken wheelbarrows of men
forming flags, waving the spokes, the unspoken
labor. The violence, of course.

Sometimes, prayer.

| questionnaire : foreclosure

I want to see your promises arranged
like shoes walking somewhere.
I never milled the sacred wheat
where the buffalo knelt
in the rotting fields of gold. I saw them
charging in my sleep. Spirits of hoof
& froth. A past of milk was
described to me when I lingered
over the empty boxes on the test,
the blanks blank-hearted &
blinking. I saw breasts
everywhere, turned inward
with the burden of energy.
There was a rush of gold,
avalanche of fame,
termites of celebrity,
they were all in the high
hills, the backwoods,
devouring pine needles. Suicides. Champagne.
This sort of language denied everything.
The signs behind the signs trembled
when the paintbrush was tossed
into the woods, the paint bucket
kicked into the middle
of the interstellar belt.

| ambition

the birds fell
dead in our front yards
new crosses of agnostics
our father who art plagued
we chewed the barred
owls' wings
they fell into our pulpits
bald plucked dipped
heathen drunk in oil they fell
eyeless in the sand
they were at whole foods
falling into bags of rice
imported GMO
we can't outgrow
ourselves
whatever the buzzards
leave of claw

the great eagle

| gun minor, or the inconsolable constellation

The bullets in America are not thoughtful. They do not go missing.
They are not tied to chairs. They are not held captive in mobile homes.
They do not announce revolution. They are a riotous amendment.
They are not walking along the bike road, offering their metal eyes
or hungry flesh to strangers. They do not ask for healthy hot lunch or medicine.
They are not being sold behind the school. They are not playing
games they learned from adults. They do not pray to gods or American idols.
We do not drain lakes or books to save them. They do not bear
their captor's children in basements. They have rights.

⁓

One day, the throat of the sky swallows itself
& the rain. In Chicago, along a blush of memory,
sad as a black girl's cheek, a word troubles
a puddle of rain where the water rolls to blood.

We give ourselves too much. Our skin
inked with slain flowers, unripe
brackets of years.

⁓

I don't want to write the word Hope
on a headstone. I don't want to count the splinters

in a child's cheek. I don't want to tell my son
to leave the hooded sweatshirt
at home.

~

Which children remembered
they could never be children again?

The ones who could look back
& watch the blackbirds nod?
The ones who could explain
why the cherry robins fell to earth
with breasts as red & hollow
as love?

~

Middle of one morning I wake up
humming *Hadiya, Hadiya.* When did your breathing
become less than birdsong? I'm smashed
across borderless sidewalks, beak
slanted to dead sky.

Her favorite color is Purple. Tell God
her favorite color is purple.

~

Our mothers sit inside, listening
to the radio, ironing all the armor
they have always prepared. Empty

glass bowls wait for our screams.
The silence shatters each day.
Our mothers watch, their eyes
mutely matching the world's work.

At the ledge of sirens,
the fathers wait, hands raised
like defeated clouds.

~

The eyes of your killers are dry.
The eyes of your killers are dry.

~

A flag with twenty-six stars folds
over the finish line in Boston. The innocent race,
the small desks silent on their sides
shine in American sunlight.

These words will start no war. Syllables
will only explode the tongue
while history assassinates bone. Remember,
the girl who ran toward us
years ago from Vietnam begging us
to promise her skin
anything
but amnesia.

Unmoored from sternum, wireless, the cuneiforms
scattered. Chameleons of culture run toward
unspeakable elements. The heart's ellipses.
Our letters slip over each other, away
from the gaslight, candle, enlightenment.
The gallows of gigabytes. An aviary of volume.
Decisions to delete. What we need space to be.
Why don't we buy more? Freeze the selves
who wait for us, their eyes poking the dark.
The grass-fed head in the icebox. The glacier
in the body urges silence, cracking bones.
Whose civilization? Whose wheel & tools?
Upon the threshing floor the imaginarium.
Man is fire, the brain's peal.
There is a deity near the window. Who
made that creature & what does it want
looking at me that way?

| dear America

I pick you up
& you are a child made of longing
clasped to my neck. Iridescent,
lovely, your inestimable tantrums,
I carry you back & forth
from the famine in your mind.

Your alphabet wraps itself
like a tourniquet
around my tongue.

Speak now, the static says.

A half-dressed woman named Truth
tells me she is a radio.

I'm going to ignore happiness
& victory.
I'm going to undo myself
with music.

I pick you up
& the naked trees lean
into the ocean where you arrived,

shaking chains & freedom
from your head.

No metaphor would pull you
out of your cage.

Light keens for the dead.
& I'm troubled
by my own blind touch.

Did the ocean release
my neck? Did the opal waves
blow our cries to shore?

You don't feel anything
in the middle of the night.

| *gymnopédie*

So it is to be Sadness,
pulling the traces of sounds
against lips
that do not respond to trouble.
The earth is open.
A theater, I once slipped through aisles of desire
& turnstiles of grainy delight. Was there
a secret photograph
of your face insisting behind the rain
you were innocent?

We were not innocent.
I was holding onto what?
Look at the playground
swinging the dark of children.

I woke up, stretching from the slur
of memory. Shivering near the water,
I lifted my mouth, slack as rope.
Is faith bellowed or hissed?
What you did to me
can't be concealed in the water.
The sunken love.
We watched the bleeding ibis
pour red through the clouds

until it turned away, disappointed
by our songs.

Faith might be that way
with suffering.

When the rain slides its clarity
into me, I am an opal. I am this flash
of city, this pelvis of omens & reprieves,
this antic blurt of water turning
like a voice.

The underdogs of night urge me
to grasp every shadow within my reach
& hold my face away
from mirrors. I break the features
into equal parts. The nightjars
feed before the owl's shudder.

Only then can I imagine how light breaks
over the earth & does not forgive
its innocence.

| 33 ages for solitude

Are you the kind of music
that claims life & death?
Never anonymous, are you
the square of rain or light?
Are you the casket or the bed?
Are you the Maybe & the Maybe Not?
Are you the word I uttered
in the dark,
in the dark, where you had no border?
O Lord, will you ever leave
the dark? Will you ever tire
of your exquisite inventions?
O likeness, the sea & creatures
who tread the earth. The music
I heard when I knelt down
in the middle of a dream
& begged to stay a dream
forever. Speak to me sometimes
in your voices of gray.
Write the world
as a clear chord in this body
you blew from mud.
Are you the kind of joy that is long?
Say that some infinity ago I knew
sweetness before I tore it away.

Are you tooth, pulling my stray music
into your cavity of granite?
Say it harder, what I have said to death:
once I loved you.
Let me be a silent sky above you now.
Let me be a 33-year-old bowstring, a
tooth,
the oak's work song, a time & root
promised to end.

| a dry run : American Caesura

Our skulls repeat as a pattern
of wallpaper. A station of late & departing
bones. We're inside the windows we're loaned.
We arrive in crowds, arresting music.
Delight knocks on wood for luck,
the front door on its hinge.
We recall the ecstasy of disorder.
Give us some news. The tripwire
has nothing to do when we don't move.
The integrity of nostalgia dissolves
like a face. The days are heaped
behind the house. In the yard alone the oak
yields to a small bruise of lightning.
The illicit sincerity some give
to the world. Eat our cinders.
We're millionaires of absence.
Inside of shoebox houses we burn
before we're dead. We watch movies
where trains never stop
chasing mountains. The whisper of
a joy we could not save. Remove the feeding tube
& say farewell. We want an ocean view
from our crypt of hopes. We gather
under the earth in a cluster of caves.

Urchins, orphaned & wordless in our work.
The soil asserts desire & the dying bees
tend silent flowers.

| The Human Zoo

"The world goes by my cage and never sees me."

—Randall Jarrell

Recuerdo: Primal Art

I was an object sometimes. With no sensible need but to be used, believed. Whose surface attracted light like a relic on a master's shelf. I rocked within until I fell over, breaking in blood on my indigenous side. Hand-painted, forged in beauty. Something you noticed during your travels & insisted your guests observe for themselves. *Touch it for yourselves*, you offered, watching their mouths wink. When you look at me you forget the hands that gave me away. You forget whether you cut those hands off & took them too, placing them inside an opposite case of glass where we will never be reunited. You smile & reach for me, the look of riotous gums pulled back to skull. The wilder ones laugh behind unpainted masks. You walk naked in the forest, daring your own hunger. The pleasure of acquisition brings you something you have nowhere to display.

The Human Zoo

The snout of solitude finds me again in a room
filled with glassy, marigold light. The dullness
of my interior bowed by hunger. The squalls
where melancholy shudders like a house
on a ridge of loam. Orphaned iambi
bleat in the stalls. Shorn by light.
Their tongues slaughtered & nailed
to the white walls. I don't know which
tongue is mine. Look through the glass again.
Animal? Or am I the work of a tool
scraping the mud floor? Half bags
of feed torn at my mouth.
My guests tap the window, wanting
to witness the rites. So many flies
I know I'm getting too close
to what I was told I would find
in the end.

About Progeny

I remember how the stars suffused
my father's life. His hands broke
the night—it was an oar. The darkness
where we rowed inside a dead window.
What should you say of the heart
these days? It is everlasting snow.
It is the mountain without doors.
It is the sky, setting with oblivion. The shore
offers no distance. A horse's dream
hunts my throat. The locution of
desire? I climbed inside wallpaper
blued with blue roses & waited.
My mind danced
like a shoe. The human party continued.
Inside of night I galloped,
pulling my name. My wooden face
& chestnut belly where the horsemen
slept one hundred years. Silvered by elegies &
myths, I remembered
the spinning wheel of lies.
The blurred anatomy of questions:
how to end this gesture?
How will the affair be squared?
How will I be shattered?
The emptiness of vowels & dignity

corroded by rain. Remember
how our grief slipped through
my eyes, hungry for nothing
& the wide fields the horses'
mouths once knew?

Uses for Silver

How I looked
from a distance: the color
of an animal forced to embrace love.
When they removed my collar
I did not run. The hunter acquired my profile
for his trophy room. My liver was painted
gold & hung from a sterling chain
in his daughter's mind. He urged arrows
inside my belly & my lungs.
Near thunder I fell, breaking
at the wrists. My ardor for the fields
& the stream where I drank long
foams of champagne vanished.
I want to see my maggots
reverse the promise of absence,
of memory. Say, the flesh
returned & my breath was again
a wild nettle of silver
each winter. The tongue
staggered far from my broken
neck. You broke it twice.
To be sure. To feel it was true.

Come near the bald knife of mercy
& watch God shriek. What creatures
the angels must have been.
Me? I cannot cry for what
the eyes must tell you.

Self, With Praise

Yes, you are now here. I can see you
because you are mine. My soaring
& my failures. You are no longer
a stranger, uninvited & welcome
to vandalize my thoughts
with the language of a woman
who does not know she is
a feast. Dear lover, the earth
meets inside of me, my wife
& my husband at once. My all,
you—sweet self of trouble
& kindness. I adore the lips
who no longer need
to imagine a future
where I am better.

The Human Zoo

The peacocks walk along the path between the black trees. They are mystics, dripping with the restraint of beauty. They duck from our gaze, refuse our diamond alleluias, do not encourage touch & we say they are free because they are not in cages. We are happy to repeat this. One male turns his head, the civil crest trembles at our approach. His train of eyes opens like a tree. Unblinking in the face of our overture, he does not admire his emerald-blue life during visiting hours. He does not hide his lack of interest.

The Skin I Live In

A tiger enters the great house. Glorious as the striped morning & as wild. Contained for centuries, the tiger tears paper whites to snow before it enters the household. Flower-breasts & flower-memory. The man who wears animal leaves shit, gold, & mud. He carries his polite prison inside the snarl of his eyes. Aching in power. Loneliness is the resinous tooth in its mouth. He remembers gardens, iron bars, blood. Say it is a man if you must. If you must know that you are trying not to say the words he forced into your morning prayers. The tiger passes through the kitchen, biting its mother who raised it. The educated fangs curve in light as he mounts the steps of time. Unaccompanied, say it is not the animal deferring to another prison. The flank heaves, ripe with iron, sorrow, sperm. A crest of white at its throat. The dark sack holds his heart in peril. Through the eyes of the aggrieved the attack is familiar. Our ordinary life calcified by the clarity & prowl of God. Fastened to the narrative of thunder & burning, the tiger is our hero to distract & distance us from our meat. He opens the door where a woman waits on all fours. Claws on breasts. Flowers in the mirror.

Elegy

You took away the night over the garden wall & left no shelter
for the aster or the deer that hid there, feeding. You emptied

the buckets where rain would last for days. Where the sparrows
bathed, blotting our raised voices against sunrise. We would walk

into this garden when the house asked us to stop fighting.
We would walk, arms crossed, fists like new bulbs turning

in mud. Turning in the dark. In the dark the scent
of lavender was unbearable. You walk away from this. You

drag my face beneath your arm. The door sighs. Without skin
I return to the house. Hold my radio near the open windows.

Inside my head my light blue head turned away on the pillow.
I'm learning how to be a shadow. I must understand

how static works. Already mysterious,
you liked that mostly until the delusions bored both of us.

The kind of breathing we did could move the moon
back to dusk. A gibbous farewell before we blamed star-fall.

You saw my silhouette in the house the way movies use tricks
to invent memories we can recognize

        (Words we repeat from an uncomfortable script)

but never had. The better things in us
tried to stay up, night after night, when the dew of illusions froze.
Even shame could be celestial.

And a new planet, like a dab of shimmers, glimpsed us. Hanging low
near the hill, I sometimes hid there, holding diamonds

& my face in my hands until it closed beneath stones,
to get away from us.

The Human Zoo

During the tour the woman used too many adjectives. She moved her hands through air. The children ate candy, half-listening. The sugar edged the superlatives when she suggested the animals were sweet-tempered. She was not a woman their mothers would have liked. Why had they been left alone with her? She walked them past the monkey house & the melancholic den of lions blinking in warped light. She pointed out the penguins & took the children to the petting zoo where she laughed to herself—a mourning dove, clipped & silent, upon her palm. "*They mate for life*," she began & then stopped. She cried when one of the goats nipped her. Making no noise, she brushed the strand of pain away, which clung to her lips like a smudge. The children petted her, tickled her with pungent straw, & later told their mothers that the woman was nice after all.

Somewhere

I turn into every shadow I've ever been,
stare at them until they form another
      woman. Celestial in her narrow blossom:
the brain stem, the spine, the ticking
hammer crowned by nipple, classical
as a fig. I'm abundant. I'm too hungry to
grieve the slanted shapes falling. The stars
shine like hooks over the flat land.
In the dark a cactus grazes my arm.
I touch the woman's shoulder of flames. I pull
her waist of night toward me. We rock
above the howls of the tribe. The coyotes
move off, answering the hunger,
the syncopated swing
of brush & self—
      torture, the embrace of two
motherless women, pouring blood
into a basin of memory.
Brightness in the dark, *please*
believe something.

(Texas, 2011)

Dusk, Monochrome

With no color but the hue
of fog—the husk of air
clustered in its dew-drenched
shroud. To the bodiless edges of
the horizon, all was gray
& white. Along the coast
I walked. Beneath life's
glaring veil with no place
breaking open to reveal
my face. Another grave
of light inscribed
with anonymity &
the mute trumpets.
This evening I have no shadow
or flight. Birds go home.
Nothing dark enough to trail
or follow. The light darkening
from the lamp on the other side
of absence. Looking over the abyss
I perceive a city of sable women

lifting their sleek pelts up
to the Pacific sea.
Their ingots of eyes & gazes,
their brooding in wet darkness
& salt. Down along the spine
of the shore, near the edge,
near the dusk & its crashing.
Their eyes empty me.
Ghosted, translucent,
a wave lifts us above
the world & flings me back
without a blink. The seals watch.
Their bodies bobbing up
through the water like black drops
of blood from the depth
of a slight wound. Following
the body the way blood follows
its wounds. No place breaking
open to brighten
the darkest look of animals.

(*Limantour Beach, California, 2011*)

114

The Human Zoo

Soon I appear through the fog, my face presses against the cage. There is a scrim of dark edging the metal. You are there, pushing life toward my mouth with your fingers. Now I reach without biting. In the dark my own hands grasp how small & tame I am. You say, *stay wild with your eyes & ideas*. But imagine if my hand could not find your hand. Through the skin of what has survived. If I come up for air but then slip again beneath the current, remember how I glittered, with water pouring from every pore. You would walk down into our earth & watch me race behind the captive green glass. I leave you the gills of my faith, the jaw of my empathy. The flowers will remember my rain & my murmurs. How absurd I am. Even the thunderheads will remember a woman who shook with fire. You sink my net to the floor & work fast. It is how we must perform kindness. My flesh opens like a black claw. Why are you still not afraid of me? I want to see how close the sun will near the water. How the end will hold a woman's wings above the flames.

Self Portrait, With Decay

With moss, the deer who stood against
the twilight in a Vermont road,
with white-capped dawns pushed
by terror, with an oval face
tilted on a pillow of childhood,
with blood pouring from her nose & mouth,
with her wedding dress, with bare feet,
with marquees announcing the end
of a woman,
with the man who could not tell the truth,
with sand dollars on a sill, with hip-stalk
& lipstick, with house party &
repast, with a bank of snow,
with sorrow & cinnamon,

with a mule being led
to the old river, with soft eyes
for her mother & father,
with a venomous apple of mistakes,
with tears & sighs in sunlight,
with a wagging stray at her heels,
with her shovel & harmonica,

with a kingdom given
away, with her two-step & moonwalk,
with hot hands on her waist,
with the laughter of her brothers & sister,
with lots of butter & salted caramel,
with the elegy of her own
laughter, with paint & seashells,
with her captive harp
of memory,

with flies hurrying after
her carcass of shame,
with the man who rubbed her
mind with hope, with bruises
of light inflicted
by imagination, with letters
& dusty diaries, a skin

embroidered
by flaws & ecstasy,
with her brindled fluke
that crashed into the joy
of an undiminished
mystery

The Human Zoo

At the gates there is a figure believed to be a man. Placed upon a pedestal his head is raised & turned as though he is speaking quietly to something behind him. As though he is listening for permission from the stone he is. There are shadows neither sunlight nor moonlight can reach. *It changes nothing*, Rilke says eventually, inside of the sun that grazes clouds of stone. At the base this man is always naked, creating the very minute he himself has named and understood as Time Lost. There are shining parts the mouth cannot reach. *Is there another pose*, the torso of solitude begs his companions. Where is the one named Woman? Thighs stoned by vandals near the north exit. Her brow a nest. The caretakers wish to explain the state of the matter. Their faces are pushed to the ledge of words. The smell of captive animals drags its truth beneath the breeze. The visitors pose here, the monkey house first & ape the sapiens. There is always a child who lingers to look up at the forlorn architecture of the man: calf, waist, & ribs, the throat, & the stone that the man has borrowed from a quarry for his face. It is the child who will ask, "Who built him?" The murmur from adults will differ. The animals bellowing the truth will not be translatable. Or, or. The child will say something better that will make the pigeons grin & enjoy their handouts. Alone, the light bursts the child's eyes for an instant. She can now observe the indelicate curse someone has inflicted, in red lipstick, near the man's heel. The verb & lightning of this word. She rubs our scar.

Notes

"Woman to Lightning" is written for the poet Ai and includes the line, "I've got the scars to prove it," from her poem, "Woman to Man."

"My Dress Hangs There" takes part of its title from Frida Kahlo's painting *My Dress Hangs There, 1933.* The poem is dedicated to Jaime Shearn Coan.

"The Reckoning of Relics" is dedicated to Tracy K. Smith. This poem is also an extended note of my gratitude to the Millay Colony in Austerlitz, New York.

"July 13, 1954" is the date of Frida Kahlo's death. The beginning of this poem references Kahlo's actual cremation. According to many stories, when Kahlo was cremated, her body suddenly sat upright, her hair blazing with flames, due to a blast of heat from the incinerator doors.

"Home, A Photograph" is an ekphrastic poem based on a series of images by Ralph Eugene Meatyard.

"July 22, 2012" is dedicated to my father and my paternal grandmother, Peggy S. Strauss Griffiths (1925 -2012). The lines "[…] there is no place / that does not see you." is taken from "Archaic Torso of Apollo" by Rainer Maria Rilke.

The poem, "Self, Traction," is based upon a photograph taken of Frida Kahlo by Nikolas Muray in 1940. This poem is dedicated to the work of Ana Mendiata, Francesca Woodman, and Pascale Petit.

"26" is dedicated to the community and extended community of Newtown, Connecticut. It is dedicated to the immeasurable and continuous loss of children to gun-related deaths.

"Woman, New Delhi" is dedicated to the memory of the 23-year-old young woman and her male friend who were attacked on December 16, 2012 in the Munirka neighborhood of New Delhi. After being brutally gang-raped and tortured, she died thirteen days after her injuries. This poem is dedicated to the millions of women who continue to be sexually assaulted and killed in every continent.

"Elegy" and "Anti-Elegy" are dedicated to Trayvon Martin, Michael Dunn, Jordan Davis, James Byrd Jr., Sean Bell, Ousmane Zongo, and too many others to include in this small book.

"Before Blood After Honey" is dedicated to those women who have died or currently face the loss of their lives due to the tradition and observation of "honor killings."

"Human Ceremony with Watermelon Sugar" was inspired by the 30 Americans exhibit. The poem is dedicated to the extraordinary painter Noah Davis.

"The Year in Pictures" uses a photograph of the Rana Plaza collapse, "Savar Dhaka, Bangladesh, April 24, 2013" by Taslima Akhter as its genesis. The titles from two of his collections, *Solitudes Crowded With Loneliness* and *The Ancient Rain* belong to Bob Kaufman. The lines: "Forgotten, as if you never were / a person, or a text . . . forgotten" and "Forgotten, as if you never were / news, or a trace . . . forgotten" belong to Mahmoud Darwish. The line "Nothing to be gained here" is taken from a painting, "Riddle Me This, Batman," by Jean-Michel Basquiat. The penultimate stanza uses a wedding portrait, by Nina Berman, of a bride and disfigured groom, Marine Sgt. Ty Ziegel, who served in Iraq and was brutally disfigured.

The poem, "a word of rescue from the great eyes," takes its title from a line in Muriel Rukeyser's "Poem as Mask." The lines "she could see the peril of an / unexamined life. / she closed her eyes, afraid to look for her / authenticity / but the light insists on itself in the world;" are taken from Lucille Clifton's poem "the light that came to lucille clifton." The section of the poem that includes these lines, "The lamp of the body is the eye. It follows that if your eye is clear, your whole body will be filled with light," is taken from Matthew 6:22-23. The poem also references the film, *Melancholia*, directed by Lars von Trier (2011) and *Gravity*, directed by Alfonso Cuarón (2013). This poem is dedicated to my paternal great-grandmother, Lucille McKay, to the spirit of Lucille Clifton, Muriel Rukeyser, and to the women, past, present, and future who challenge and support me.

The section "gun minor, or the inconsolable constellation" is dedicated to Hadiya Pendleton (1998-2013), Christian Choate (1996-2009), Anjelica Castillo ("Baby Hope," 1987-1991), Deonta Howard, Hailey Dominguez, Khalise Witherspoon, and victims of the 2013 Boston Marathon Bombing.

"The Skin I Live In" takes much of its imagery as well as its title from the film directed by Pedro Almodóvar (2011).

Acknowledgments

Academy of American Poets Poem-A-Day Series; Alaska Quarterly Review; American Poetry Review; At Length; Black Renaissance Noire; Black Nature: Four Centuries of African American Nature Poetry; The Boiler; CrossBronx; CURA; Ecotone; Four Way Review; Kweli Journal; Lily Literary Review; Memoria, Memoria (A5 | Deadly Chaps chapbook series); *Narrative Northeast; North American Review; PLUCK!; Reverie; REVOLUTIONesque; The Fiddleback; Tongue; Thrush Poetry Journal;* and *24Pearl*

Rachel Eliza Griffiths is a poet and visual artist. She is the recipient of fellowships including the Cave Canem Foundation, Millay Colony, Provincetown Fine Arts Work Center, and the Vermont Studio Center. Her visual and literary work has appeared widely. Griffiths is the creator and director of P.O.P (Poets on Poetry), a video series of contemporary poets featured by the Academy of American Poets. Her third collection of poetry, *Mule & Pear* (New Issues Poetry & Prose), was selected for the 2012 Inaugural Poetry Award by the Black Caucus of the American Library Association. Currently, Griffiths teaches creative writing at Sarah Lawrence College and lives in Brooklyn.

Publication of this book was made possible by grants and donations. We are also grateful to those individuals who participated in our 2014 Build a Book Program. They are:

Nickie Albert
Michele Albright
Whitney Armstrong
Jan Bender-Zanoni
Juanita Brunk
Ryan George
Michelle Gillett
Elizabeth Green
Dr. Lauri Grossman
Martin Haugh
Nathaniel Hutner
Lee Jenkins
Ryan Johnson
Joy Katz
Neal Kawesch
Brett Fletcher Lauer & Gretchen Scott
David Lee
Daniel Levin
Howard Levy
Owen Lewis
Paul Lisicky
Maija Makinen
Aubrie Marrin
Malia Mason
Catherine McArthur
Nathan McClain
Michael Morse
Chessy Normile
Rebecca Okrent
Eileen Pollack

Barbara Preminger
Kevin Prufer
Soraya Shalforoosh
Alice St. Claire-Long
Megan Staffel
Marjorie & Lew Tesser
Boris Thomas
William Wenthe